D0895510

Do's and Don'ts of Yesteryear

A Treasury of Early American Folk Wisdom

Eric Sloane

DOVER PUBLICATIONS, INC.
Mineola, New York

Copyright

Bibliographical Note

This Dover edition, first published in 2008, is an unabridged republication, in one volume, of *Eric Sloane's Do: A Little Book of Early American Know-How,* originally published by Walker and Company, New York, in 1972; and *Eric Sloane's Don't: A Little Book of Early American Gentility,* originally published by Walker and Company, New York, in 1968.

Library of Congress Cataloging-in-Publication Data

Do's and don'ts of yesteryear : a treasury of early American folk wisdom / Eric Sloane.

      p. cm.

    An unabridged republication of 2 works. 1st work originally published: Eric Sloane's Do. New York : Walker, 1972. 2nd work published: Eric Sloane's Don't. New York : Funk & Wagnalls, 1968 (originally published under the title: Don't / written by Oliver Bell Bunce).

    ISBN-13: 978-0-486-45594-5

    ISBN-10: 0-486-45594-7

    1. Recipes—United States. 2. Handbooks, vade-mecums, etc. 3. Etiquette—United States. 4. United States—Social life and customs—Miscellanea. 5. Folklore—United States. I. Sloane, Eric. Do. II. Bunce, Oliver Bell, 1828–1890. Don't.

AG105.D73 2008
398—dc22

                                       2007032510

Manufactured in the United States of America
Dover Publications, Inc., 31 East 2nd Street, Mineola, N.Y. 11501

Do

The
1800s

the
1700s

—a Foreword—

Early America was cluttered with a weary lot of "don'ts." People were so strict about not doing this and not doing that. Yet that disciplined life was also livened by an amazing number of things to do. Benjamin Franklin's warning about "idle hands getting into mischief" was intended for children but there is so little for adults to do for themselves nowadays that the self-doer is nearly obsolete and modern living has become a bore.

5

One of the first delights of life was when the child learned to button up his own pants but the zipper eliminated that satisfying exercise of dexterity. Grinding coffee, making ice cream, shining shoes, and nearly all the small movements that made up the continuous ballet of daily life a few years back are now being done by plugging into a socket or flipping a switch. Even the satisfaction of knowing where that electric power comes from is kept from us and sometimes the power company doesn't know either. I still recall the extraordinary pleasure of pumping spring water and carrying it for the household: now I turn on a faucet and I am too lazy to wonder where the stuff is coming from. Perhaps if I really knew, I wouldn't drink it. We used to pray to God for our needs to be fulfilled; now we depend upon the establishment.

Years ago when I contemplated the difference between the early American and his modern counterpart, I made some interesting finds. The old-timer was smaller, about twenty to fifty pounds lighter than the average man of today, but he was wiry and very much stronger.

Bread was as solid and hard as the people who ate it, but now the "staff of life" is as fat and spongy and full of air as we have become. The "sports fan" of today seldom does his own thing; instead, he watches others do their things, eating and drinking at the TV while sitting on a behind that would have shamed great-grandfather.

There is no doubt about it, doing things by and for ourselves has become a lost art, and the joy of doing things not just "the old-fashioned way" but plainly the right way is a nearly vanished satisfaction. Living in the country where you have to chop your own firewood, pump your own water, and do a lot of your own repairing is worth the trouble: the psychiatrists make less profit but life is seldom a bore.

On rainy days while poring through old almanacs, I used to copy down recipes and ancient household hints: trying them out was a constant game of fun. Some friends insisted I was being quaint and nostalgically precious but whenever a problem came up, I usually had the answer. I could cure hiccups, light a proper fire, mend almost anything, predict the weather, get rid of ants, swallows, bees, or boring houseguests. I could tell a fresh egg from a spoiled one, clean spots, fix broken furniture, make paint or glue or whitewash or soap, wines, herb teas, and switchel.

And not least of all, I had the making of this handy little book to be read during rainy days, chock full of things to do. Happy doing!

Eric Sloane,
Warren, Connecticut.

P.S. This haphazard, unindexed rambling of things to do, happens to be part of the format; it is just as I copied them down, just as they were in old almanacs and diaries. One book of 1785 tells "how to amputate an arm" and to "remove a gangrenous finger." In the same book, indeed only ten pages later, there are recipes for baking cookies and instructions for the best way to take rust from iron pots. That was often the way information was compiled, and like it or not, it is the way I've put this little book together.

Do

Do hammer a squared peg into a round
hole when you wish a wood joint to stay.

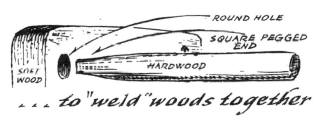

ROUND HOLE

SQUARE PEGGED
END

HARDWOOD

SOFT
WOOD

... *to "weld" woods together*

A hardwood stick, if partly squared, will
soon "weld" itself into a round-holed
softwood piece and stay tight throughout
the years.

Do use leather from old belts to make
small door hinges. Great grandfather
used two, three, or four leather pieces
on cabinet doors, using tacks or screws;
this made silent, easy swinging hinges.

11

Do hang a broom from a nail instead of resting it upon the floor. Letting a broom stand can give it a permanent warp within a few hours.

Do keep a bag of salt as a handy fire extinguisher. A chimney fire can be dealt with by shutting doors and putting salt upon the fire in the grate. Salt-formed gases tend to extinguish flames.

Do measure anything tall (such as a building or tree) by simply measuring its shadow at a given time. By placing a stick in the ground and waiting until its shadow length equals its own height, all other objects' shadows will at that instant also equal their height.

Do pack fancy frosted cakes (for mailing) in popped corn. The icing will smear less but even when it does, the icing will simply produce a sweetened popcorn, good to eat.

Do roll newspapers into rolls by wrapping them with string. A stack of these "logs" will do almost as well in your

fireplace as real wood. Newsprint is produced from wood anyway.

Do make a simple fire-maker by filling
a lard can with fireplace ashes soaked
with kerosene. Supplied with a large
spoon, this stuff starts a fire quickly. The
Indians in New Mexico still use this as
their fire-kindler.

Do before sweeping a floor, sprinkle it
with damp tea leaves or bran. This col-
lects dust and also keeps it from rising
into the room.

Do trim glass to be made round or
oval by cutting it with scissors under
water. First mark the oval with a crayon,
then with a large scissors cut the glass
while it is well submerged. Splinters are
less dangerous when kept from flying
about, but great care is still necessary.

Do clean woodwork marred by match-
scratching etc., by rubbing it with half
a lemon. Fingermarks will also disappear
by this method.

Do try the simplest of sickroom disinfectants—a plate full of sliced onions.

Do bottle a good woodwork cleaner by saving tea leaves and steeping them in a tin pail for about half an hour. This also washes windows and mirrors with a harmless detergent effect.

Do instead of removing burned-down candle stubs, just place a new candle on the still burning stub. Pressing a new candle over the old stub will firm it in place and save both time and wax.

Do use charcoal as a superb toothcleaner and breath-freshener. Second best is salt, then bicarbonate of soda, all three have been used for centuries. Benjamin Franklin made a mixture of honey and pulverized charcoal for whitening the teeth. Another tooth cleaner recipe was: take a pound of soft water, two ounces of lemon juice, six grains of burnt alum and the same of salt. Boil them for a minute, then strain and bottle for use. Dip a small sponge in this and rub the teeth once a week for removing stains.

Do clean windows with damp news-paper. The ink actually aids in cleaning and the paper is unusually absorbent.

Do keep corrugated cardboard boxes for storing things. Boxes of kindling are easier to pile than loose sticks. A corru-

ROPE
KNOT

Cardboard boxes slide anywhere

gated box on the end of a rope makes a fine sled for small children sliding over snow, grass, or land.

Do make candles burn slower (as when a night light is needed) by putting salt on top till it reaches the black part of the wick. In this way the smallest candle can be made to last longer with a steady, mild light.

Do treat infection by piling a pinch of Epsom salts on the infected spot, covering with a bandage, and wetting well. Overnight the infection will be drawn to a head and the surrounding skin soft and fresh.

Do discourage flies by putting out a plate containing half a teaspoon of black pepper, a teaspoon of brown sugar, and a teaspoon of cream. This strange recipe of the 1700's has no logic but seems to work.

Do beat eggs quicker by adding a pinch of salt. Salt cools eggs and produces a quicker froth.

Do move heavy objects (such as an icebox, trunk, etc.) by tipping it onto a broom. Another person pulling the broom-handle, the heaviest object may be slid across the floor with ease.

Do tighten sagging cane-bottom chairs by turning them upside down and sponging the cane with hot soapy water; then dry in the sun. Sagging will soon disappear.

Do (in building a house) try fitting the doorframe to the door instead of fitting a door into a doorframe. Even a warped door can be perfectly fitted if it is hung or put in place and the frame built around it. No alterations are needed; it's how the early builders did it.

Do restore withered flowers by plunging the stems into boiling water. By the time the water is cooled, the flowers will have been revived. With stems cut off and left to stand in cold water, they should then keep for several days.

Do split elm logs by slicing them around the sides. An axe stuck into the center of an elm log will become locked in place, and not split the log.

Do stain floors with permanganate of potash (drugstores have it) with a quarter ounce to the quart of water. Repeat to darken. At first the color will be bright magenta, but it will soon turn a proper dark brown.

Do use your outstretched arms to measure a room, etc. Fingertip to fingertip your armspread will equal your exact height. Try it and see.

DO

Do make a simple soap by using potatoes three-fourths boiled and then mashed. This not only cleans hands as well as common soap but it prevents winter chap and makes the hands soft and healthy.

Do clean oil paintings with a paste of soft wood ashes and white wine. Quickly add olive oil before wetness soaks into the paint, and use only small amounts.

Do banish odor of onions on the breath by chewing fresh walnuts or a few raw parsley leaves.

Do clean and polish knives with fireplace ashes.

Do unwarp boards with wetness and/or heat. Wood, cardboard or other panels expands on its wet side (or heated side) curling downward. Simply wet or heat the opposite side for a while, and the board will straighten. A board curled from laying on the ground will straighten simply by reversing it (still on the ground) until the warp disappears.

Do know the Weather

Do know the weather and predict it the old fashioned way. For example, a heavy dew at night foretells a clear morrow; a dry night lawn predicts rain on the morrow. When smoke rises quickly, good weather prevails, but when smoke curls downward and lingers near the fire, a storm awaits. Lightning appearing from a western quadrant (southwest, west, or northwest) is from a storm which will reach you, but from any other direction, it is from a storm which will not reach you. A halo around the sun or moon (except in mid-winter) foretells a long, slow precipitation within ten hours. The slower and longer a storm takes to reach you, the longer it will last. Birds flying particularly high indicate cool dry air and good weather.

20

Do make New England glazed white-wash by taking two gallons of water, a pound and a half of rice and a pound of moist sugar. Let this mixture boil until the rice is dissolved, then thicken it to a proper consistency with finely powdered lime. This whitewash gives a lasting satiny finish seen in the earliest farm-house walls. By adding milk or eggs the paint becomes plastic and more lasting.

Do make black paint from an ancient recipe by baking potatoes (first slowly and then briskly) until they are com-pletely burned or charred. This black powder ground well in linseed oil pro-duces a fine black paint.

Do stop coughing from a cold by roast-ing a large lemon (without burning it): when thoroughly hot, cut and squeeze it into a cup over three ounces of finely powdered sugar. Take a spoonful to stop the cough. Another ancient remedy is a boiled concoction of sugar-water and pine tree leaves. Plain hoarseness is re-lieved by a syrup of fresh-scraped horse-radish and twice its weight in vinegar.

Do insure stability with three legs instead of four on tables and benches. Outdoor pieces, small benches, and candle stands were always made with three legs so they would not wobble or upset on old-time uneven floors.

Do pick special apples to be kept for a long while, with cotton gloves. The oil from human hands hastens decay. Lay apples in hay rather than a hard basket, as the slightest bruise also hastens decay.

Do discourage ants by placing cucumber rind shavings wherever they appear.

Do handle fine firearms touching only the wooden parts. Each fingerprint will become a rust spot in time.

Do cure a head cold and hoarseness of the throat with gruel (or oatmeal) made in the regular way: when nearly ready, slice in two or three onions and simmer it for twenty minutes. Pour in a lump of butter with pepper and salt. Eat this with bread and butter (if you are that hungry) before retiring.

Do keep potatoes from sprouting by placing an apple amongst them. The legend is that above-ground plants do not grow together with below-ground plants, and the presence of the above-ground fruit paralyses the growth of the potato.

Do make early American "kitchen red" paint by mixing Indian red or powdered red earth mixed with black from a lamp and binded with sour milk. Milk was a source of the earliest paints and its lasting quality founded the first plastic paints.

Do water newly planted trees by boring holes near the roots, filling holes with water once a week for a month.

Do divide anything into any number of irregular parts by using a ruler. By simply slanting your ruler and still using the inch measurements, you get even more accurate measurements than using arithmetic. For example, it seems difficult to divide a board ten and three-sixteenth inches wide into six parts. But by slanting a one-foot ruler from one side of the board to the other, and then dividing the twelve-inch ruler into six parts, you solve the problem without arithmetic.

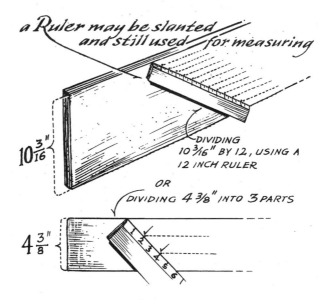

a Ruler may be slanted and still used for measuring

$10\frac{3}{16}"$

DIVIDING $10\frac{3}{16}"$ BY 12, USING A 12 INCH RULER

OR

DIVIDING $4\frac{3}{8}"$ INTO 3 PARTS

$4\frac{3}{8}"$

Do cure wounds in trees with a paste made of a fourth of lime (old plaster or lime rubbish ground fine will do), a fourth wood ashes, a fourth sand, and a fourth of cow dung. Cow dung alone was also used.

Do dry towels in the sun after washing them. Even after ironing wet towels, the slightest dampness evolves into a minute but dangerous mold which is banished by the sun's rays. The old-timers placed their towels on green bushes to dry.

Do keep apples very much longer by not allowing one apple to touch the other. For keeping special apples throughout a winter, wipe them dry and pack them in sawdust, dry sand, or charcoal; then put them in a cool place.

Do ease earache by removing the heart of a roasted onion and placing it into (but not too far) the ear. A stick of green walnut or hickory laid on a fire till the sap ran out the end produced a liquid that early doctors dropped into infected ears. A vinegar and salt wash applied warm was also used.

Do make a good and simple easel for painting by using a ladder. A folding ladder makes a sturdy easel by putting nails at the proper height to hold your canvas or board.

Do put fenceposts into the ground root-end up to prevent rotting. Charring that part to go underground will further prevent damprot.

Do keep salt flowing during damp weather by placing a small cube of soft wood in the salt cellar.

Do remember that the oldest, cheapest, and best toilet powder is simple kitchen starch. You may perfume it to taste with aromatic flowers or herbs pressed into the starch between folded paper.

Do try the oldest recipe for fine hair shampoo and hair softener. Just beat up a fresh egg and rub it into the hair. It sounds messy and takes four washes to complete the shampoo, but it is effective.

Do see objects easier in the dark by looking to just one side of the object. Try looking at a faint star (you can stare it into invisibility); then look to just one side of the star and see it suddenly come into the clearest view.

Do make clothes hooks or shelf brackets from small tree crotches. The old-timers knew that the strongest part of wood was the crotches of stems, so that is how they made their harness hooks and shelf brackets.

a natural Bracket and Hook

Do keep a bottle of handy spot-remover made of salt and lemon and water. Wet stained cloth with this and allow the material to dry in sunlight. This is also a fine hand conditioner.

Do tell a hard-boiled egg (or a bad egg) from a fresh egg by spinning it. The fresh egg will not spin but wobble to a stop.

Do cure quinsy sore throat with bicarbonate of soda. Make a paper funnel, put a small pinch of powder inside, aim it at the lower throat, and get someone to blow into the funnel.

Do make your own furniture polish. Here are five old-time recipes: 1. A pint bottle filled with equal parts of linseed oil and kerosene; apply with one flannel, dry with another. 2. One pint of linseed oil and a small glass of gin, add half a pound of treacle (sugar-house molasses). If rubbed dry, the shine is remarkable. 3. Three parts linseed oil and one part turpentine; apply with one flannel and dry with another. 4. Mix boiling linseed oil with white varnish (one-fourth varnish and three-fourths oil). 5. One-third vinegar and one-third sweet oil and one-third spirits of wine; shake well and keep for a while.

Do exterminate crawling insects with powdered borax. Another way is to put alum into hot water and boil till it dissolves; then apply to cracks, etc. with no danger to pets or humans.

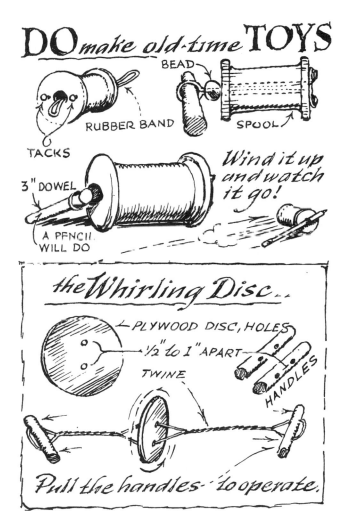

DO *make old-time* TOYS

BEAD

RUBBER BAND

TACKS

SPOOL

3" DOWEL

A PENCIL WILL DO

Wind it up and watch it go!

the Whirling Disc...

PLYWOOD DISC, HOLES
1/2" to 1" APART

HANDLES

TWINE

Pull the handles—to operate.

Do get rid of swallows in barns or garages by placing a stuffed owl there. The result is instantaneous and swallows will never return.

Do relieve bee stings with table salt (rubbed into the sting). Ammonia is second best. If neither is available, use mud.

Do remember that house plants enjoy many human foods. Leftover fish, coffee grounds, water from boiled eggs, crushed eggshells, water from cooked foods, watered milk, all give plants a lift. The effects of shrimp is best of any plant reviver.

Do relieve toothache with cloves (powdered or whole).

Do make old-time black schoolroom ink. Half an ounce of logwood and ten grains of bichromate of potash dissolved in a quart of hot rain water. When cold, put into a bottle for a week when it will be ready for use.

Do make a child's hammock from abandoned barrel staves. Placing the staves between separated rope about

a barrel stave Hammock

two inches apart, a serviceable swinging hammock will result to please the children.

Do hide valuables or cash to protect it from fire while you are away from home for a short while by placing it in a cellophane bag and putting in the freezer. It will be well-hidden and in about the last place to melt from heat. The idea is older than you might think: farmers used to keep paper money in their cold cellars or in the wellhouse, hence the reference to "cold cash."

Do tell where the nearest low pressure area (storm) is located. Just face the wind and hold out your right hand, pointing to your right; you will be pointing toward the nearest storm area. By doing this you can follow the eye of a hurricane as it moves along.

Do build a stump puller or "log jack." Small bushes or tree stumps may be lifted from the earth (in wet weather) by means of a short round log through which has been put an iron rod (a hickory or ash stick might do). A rope used to be used to pull the iron rod, using ox power.

to Pull a Stump

Do make a Paul Revere barn lantern by punching holes in a lard can and putting a candle inside. A good outside

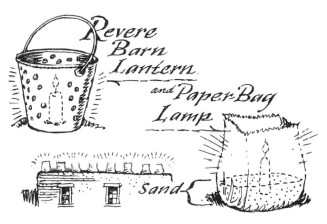

Revere Barn Lantern and Paper-Bag Lamp

Sand

lantern to light a doorway (or for decoration) may be made by partially filling a paper bag with sand and inserting a candle in the bag. In Mexico, Christmas Eves were lit by hundreds of these "candlerias" outlining each house.

Do remove white spots (from hot dishes) on a table by pouring kerosene on the spot, rubbing hard with soft cloth; then pour a bit of wine on it and rub dry.

Do know how to make a perfect oval of any proportion. With two pins, tie a loose loop of thread or cord around them; then holding a pencil upright on the inside of the loop, describe as near a circle as you can, stretching the loop with the pencil as you go. The result will be an oval. Different distances apart of the pins and different size loops will make differently shaped ovals.

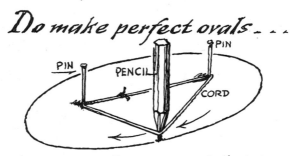

Do make perfect ovals . . .

FARTHER APART *the* PINS, THINNER *the* OVAL

Do orient yourself at night by knowing that the moon travels about the same course as the sun. A full moon, for example, is always opposite the western setting sun, so it rises in the east.

Do know how to make a five-pointed star, the same way Betsy Ross made the American flag stars to show George Washington, with a scissored piece of white paper.

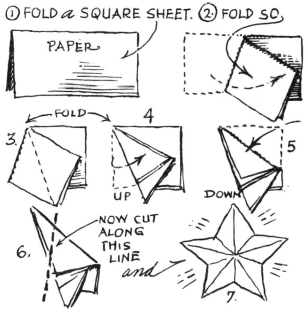

Do make a 5 pointed Star

① FOLD *a* SQUARE SHEET. ② FOLD SO,

PAPER

←FOLD→   4

3.

UP

DOWN   5

NOW CUT ALONG THIS LINE

6.   *and*

7.

DO

Do observe clouds and the sky without glare. Paint the underside of a piece of glass black, then look at the reflection of the sky from the top. This "black glass" was used by early artists when painting the sky.

Do make apple butter by stirring it continuously for at least seven hours (which seems to be the old-time trick for excellent butter). They used to use a monstrous iron pot and an eight-foot long wooden "hoe" (for stirring) to keep the farmwife from the intense heat. Mix one gallon of cider and three pounds of sugar, adding spices to taste (allspice, cloves, and cinnamon). Boil to the consistency of molasses and add this mixture to the previously peeled and cubed apples, cooking till it thickens to a creamy consistency.

Do dye your own linens. Tea grounds boiled in iron and set with copperas makes "Williamsburg slate" color. Cloth boiled in heavy tea becomes a rich cream color. Old nails or rusty iron boiled in vinegar with a small bit of alum makes a fine purple slate color. The scaly moss from rocks boiled in water for four hours makes a dye-water if cloth is then boiled till color is correct. Elderberry juice infusion produces blue, tincture of saffron (or nitrate of copperas) produces green, redwood produces red.

Do make your own dandelion wine. Three pounds of dandelion blooms (no stems), three oranges, three lemons, a cake of yeast, and three and one-half pounds of honey (same amount of sugar will substitute). Boil dandelions, oranges, and lemons in two gallons of water for twenty minutes. Let stand overnight and add yeast and sweetening. Pour into crock and cover with cloth: let stand for two weeks before bottling.

Do make simple mead by boiling three parts of water to one part honey until one-third of the mixture evaporates. Skim, pour into cask, and let stand for a week. By adding boiled raisins and brandy, lemon peel and cinnamon, a compound mead is made: cask should then be filled to top so "working" of the mead may overflow. Allow to overflow till frothing ceases, then store for three months.

DO

Do clean silver the way Paul Revere did. Simply make a paste of baking soda and scrub with a brush. A soft toothbrush will do.

Do prevent sickness from overeating or from eating the wrong food the way George Washington did, and not with the aspirin-base pills of today. Just add hot water in a glass to two teaspoonsful of honey and two teaspoonsful of vinegar.

Do know the value of a compass; a piece of string with a tack on one end and a pencil on the other is sufficient. Instead of arithmetic or a square, the old-timers made square foundations and perfectly square rooms with such a device. Collectors have often wondered why there were few rulers or squares to be found in colonial carpenters' tool kits, yet so many large and small wooden compasses. For a few examples of how the compass was used instead of arithmetic, do observe the following two pages of drawings: whereby squares, right angles, octagons, etc. can be made with a simple compass or a compass-string.

to make **Square** *with a Compass*

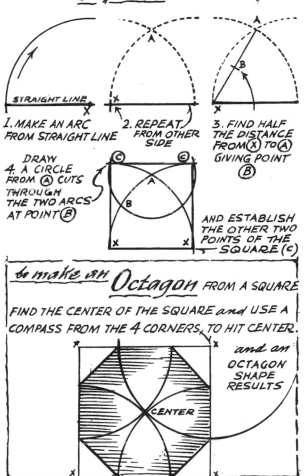

1. MAKE AN ARC FROM STRAIGHT LINE

STRAIGHT LINE

2. REPEAT. FROM OTHER SIDE

3. FIND HALF THE DISTANCE FROM (X) TO (A) GIVING POINT (B)

DRAW 4. A CIRCLE FROM (A) CUTS THROUGH THE TWO ARCS AT POINT (B)

AND ESTABLISH THE OTHER TWO POINTS OF THE SQUARE (C)

to make an **Octagon** *FROM A SQUARE*

FIND THE CENTER OF THE SQUARE *and* USE A COMPASS FROM THE 4 CORNERS, TO HIT CENTER.

and an OCTAGON SHAPE RESULTS

CENTER

to Square board with a Compass

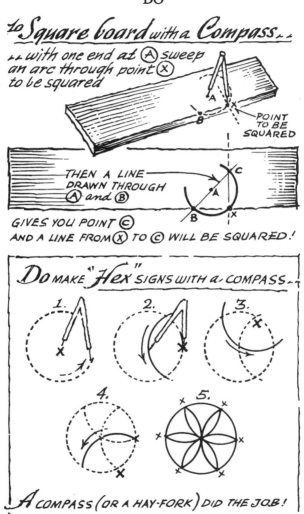

.. with one end at (A) sweep an arc through point (X) to be squared

POINT TO BE SQUARED

THEN A LINE DRAWN THROUGH (A) and (B)

GIVES YOU POINT (C) AND A LINE FROM (X) TO (C) WILL BE SQUARED!

Do MAKE "Hex" SIGNS WITH a COMPASS..

1.

2.

3.

4.

5.

A COMPASS (OR A HAY-FORK) DID THE JOB!

Do make a kitchen porch herb-barrel. Make as many large holes as you can in an old barrel, filling it with stones in the center and rich soil around the outer perimeter. Herbs planted in each hole will thrive and grow outward, being both decorative and useful near the kitchen.

Do mark special books by putting your name or initials unremovable on the bare page-ends instead of on a flat page which could be torn out. Not to be recommended, of course, for rare books.

41

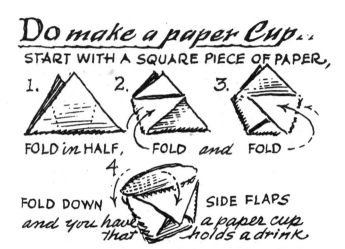

Do make a paper Cup..

START WITH A SQUARE PIECE OF PAPER,

1. 2. 3.

FOLD *in* HALF, FOLD *and* FOLD --

4.

FOLD DOWN SIDE FLAPS *and you have* a paper cup *that* holds a drink

Do make ornamental pyramids out of thick magazines. Discarded Sears and Roebuck catalogs used to be folded page by page, making colorful table decorations of fluted pages, sometimes used as doorstops. One way to use time during long winter snows, this is a slow piece of work but the result will amaze you. A small book (one hundred pages or so) will make a good file for bills, envelopes, etc.

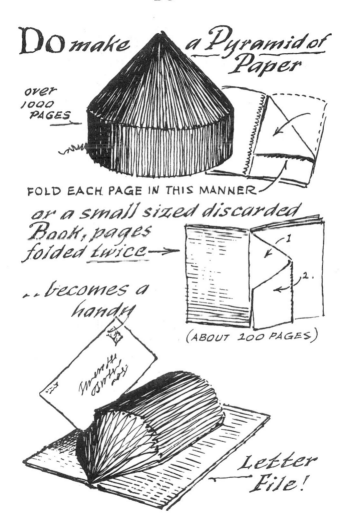

Do *make* *a Pyramid of Paper*

over 1000 PAGES

FOLD EACH PAGE IN THIS MANNER

or a small sized discarded Book, pages folded twice →

1.
2.

(ABOUT 100 PAGES)

..becomes a handy

Letter File!

Do make a boomerang with two sticks. Balsa is best, as a small, light boomerang will circle within a large room. Throw

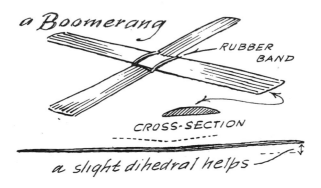

a Boomerang

RUBBER BAND

CROSS-SECTION

a slight dihedral helps

it straight ahead (as if chopping) with a downward hatchet stroke, with the curved side to your left (if you are right-handed), and throw it into the wind. It will return to your hands.

Do make the best skin toner. Make a pint of very strong mint tea, letting it steep overnight. Add one pint of pure

44

apple cider vinegar. Bottle and let stand for two days, when it will be ready for use. Do keep a rain barrel if possible, for rainwater is best for washing ladies' faces and hair.

Do take an air bath. Benjamin Franklin rose each morning at daybreak, got out of bed and passed half an hour in his chamber without any clothes. This, he said, refreshened as much as a complete bath in water.

Do make ginger wine. Five gallons of water and seven pounds of sugar and the whites of four eggs (well beaten and strained) all mixed together while cold. When it boils, skim it well and add at least a quarter pound of common white ginger; then boil for twenty minutes. Have ready the rinds of four lemons cut very thin and pour the hot liquid over them. When cool, put into a cask and add a spoonful of yeast. Next day stop the cask up and bottle within three weeks. Let bottles stand for two to three months.

Do use hay on icy steps during winter, instead of salt or sand. It won't track white spots into the house or poison vegetation. Great-grandfather used to keep a couple of bales of hay beside the farmhouse entrance and scatter a few handfuls of hay around an icy doorway.

Do make a window sundial. Few very early pioneer houses had clocks; and when a clock stopped there was no way to set it when neighbors were far away. The shadow of any upright mullion in a southerly window will cast enough of a shadow on the windowsill to indicate the passing of time, and a very thin pencil line on the sill can show several midday hours, as did many a colonial southerly windowsill.

Do make a barometer with a wide-mouthed bottle, and a piece of toy balloon rubber. By fastening a piece of rubber over the mouth of a wide-mouthed bottle, you will trap the air of the moment inside, with that exact pressure of the day. Lowering outside pressure or rising outside pressure will then expand or depress the rubber cover. By gluing a "pointer" (a long light sliver of wood or straw) to

one side of the rubber cover, the pointer will move up or down according to weather pressure-changes. This gadget must be kept from direct sunlight or other heat which might cause the air inside to expand or contract from heat or cold. Even if not very accurate, this homemade machine explains the action and mechanics of the modern aneroid barometer.

Do preserve plants from frost by treating them before being exposed to the sun or thawed. Sprinkle well with spring water in which common salt has been dissolved. Sprinkle again as the plant revives.

Do strike damp matches on glass. A rough surface will crumble match heads but a glass or other smooth surface will usually produce a flame from a damp match.

Do tell the exact temperature by counting the chirps of the common black house cricket. Count the number of chirps occurring in fourteen seconds and then add forty; the result will be the exact temperature (where the cricket is).

Do make gunpowder by mixing five parts of saltpeter with one part of sulphur and one part of charcoal. Mixed with a few drops of water in a mortar, this was rolled in paste rods the thickness of a pin, then cut into small grains and dried.

Do know that one reason for the long fringe on old-time buckskin hunting coats was that in an emergency, each piece of fringe could become a string tied together to produce a longer cord for binding to make a tourniquet or for repairing broken gear.

Do loosen rust stains with salt and lemon juice, then wash off.

Do decorate children's parties with toy balloons. By rubbing the balloon a few times, electric magnetism evolves and the balloon will stick to the wall or ceiling as if by magic. Do not leave the balloon there too long however, as the magnetism attracts dust too, and it will leave a dark ring upon the ceiling.

Do save chimney soot as an extraordinary plant manure. Mixed with a third earth and a third dung, you have a rare medicine for sick plants.

Do recognize true north as the side of a tree trunk with most moss.

Do *Know how to bind with both ends of the binding underneath.*

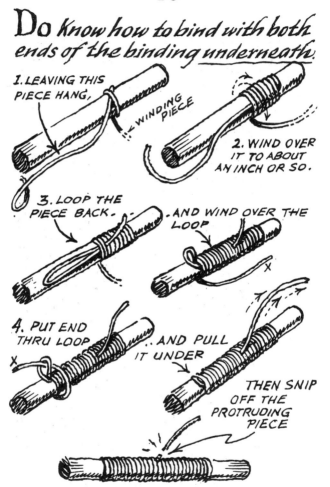

1. LEAVING THIS PIECE HANG,

WINDING PIECE

2. WIND OVER IT TO ABOUT AN INCH OR SO.

3. LOOP THE PIECE BACK.

..AND WIND OVER THE LOOP

X

4. PUT END THRU LOOP

X

..AND PULL IT UNDER

THEN SNIP OFF THE PROTRUDING PIECE

SILK·BOUND FISH·POLES WERE DONE THIS WAY.

Do ease stuck drawers or windows with common brown soap. It makes the best and longest-lasting wood lubricant.

Do *try these 1749 dessert recipes...*

PIPPIN TARTS. Pare thin, two oranges; boil the peels tender and shred fine. Core and pare twenty apples and put them in a stew pan with as little water as possible to cook. When half done add half a pound of sugar, the orange juice and the peel, and boil till thick. When cold, put in shallow dish to be eaten cold.

SYLLABUBS. Mix a quart of thick raw cream, a pound of sugar, a pint of white and a pint of sweet wine in a deep pan. Add the grated peels and the juice of three lemons. Beat or whisk it one way half an hour, then put in glasses. It will keep for ten days in a cool place.

ORANGE FOOL. Mix the juice of three oranges, a pint of cream, a little nutmeg and cinnamon, and sweeten to taste. Set the whole over a slow fire and stir till it becomes as thick as melted butter, but it must not be boiled. Pour it into a dish for eating cold.

LEMON HONEYCOMB. Sweeten the juice of a lemon to your taste and put it into a dish. Mix the white of an egg with a pint of rich cream and a little sugar; whisk it and as the froth rises, put it into the dish and over the lemon juice. Do this the day before it is to be used.

POTATO CHEESECAKES. Boil six ounces of potatoes and (separately) four ounces of lemon peel; beat the latter in a mortar with four ounces of sugar; then add the potatoes, beaten, and four ounces of butter melted in a little cream. When well mixed, let it stand to cool. Put crust in pattypans and rather more than half fill them. Bake in a quick oven half an hour. Sprinkle sugar on them when going to the oven.

SACK CREAM. Boil a pint of raw cream, the yelk (yolk) of an egg well beaten, three teaspoons of white wine, sugar and lemon peel to taste. Stir over a gentle fire till it be as thick as rich cream. Put in a dish to be served cold with rusks or sippets of toasted bread.

QUICK PUDDING. Flour and suet half a pound each, four eggs, a quarter pint of new milk, a little mace and nutmeg, a quarter pound of raisins, ditto of currants. Mix well and boil three quarters of an hour with lid on the pot.

the 1800s

the
1700s

Don't

Foreword

In this era of escape philosophy, traditional custom seems far away and appropriate only to an obsolete age. A social rebellion that accepts teen-age revolt, junk art, pornography, and hallucinatory drugs appears to have little need for the niceties of etiquette. In fact, the practice of doing the exact opposite of what grandfather used to do is now considered fashionable. Dinner clothes for men are now being worn with football-type turtleneck sweaters, decorated with beads and necklaces; mother wears exactly what young daughter wears, to the extent of featuring—often almost displaying—those parts of the body whose name used to be derived from the word "private." Broadly speaking, manners (which Webster defines as "habit, custom, fashion or mode of procedure") are fairly out of date.

As for myself, I believe that strict good manners and good breeding still have a place in the world, and the fact that you must go into the past to research this fine art fails to render it obsolete or less valuable. Mark Twain quipped that "good breeding consists in concealing how much we think of ourselves and how little we think of the other person," but Oliver Wendell Holmes, who was more serious, defined good breeding as "surface Christianity." Further back in the days when America was young, the art of being a gentleman was considered part of a Christian life, as important in schooling as reading and writing and arithmetic. No, I take that back: it was considered more important.

The simple rules of social decency and consideration for others, which we now are apt to regard as kid stuff or obsolete etiquette, were basic studies to the great men of the times. I find in my library countless books written for yesterday's school use which today's average adult would do well to read. Perhaps because of its tiny size and decorative quality I left one such book—an ancient and tattered volume, titled "DON'T"—lying on my living-room table.

"DON'T" contains no more than the simplest rules of etiquette of its time, but my guests who skim through the pages, while thoroughly enjoying and laughing at its dated style and occasional snobbishness, always remark how pertinent its contents are to present-day life. It also shocks them to realize how far we frequently stray from the simplest habits of gentleness. They have usually suggested to me the idea of reprinting this little volume, both as a curiosity and as a guide to basic manners, and although for a long while I accepted their remarks as drawing-room conversation, I finally decided to do something about it.

My publisher was as enthusiastic as my guests about "DON'T," and encouraged me to let it be reprinted. Here it is, then; sometimes amusing and reminiscent of the past, sometimes shocking—when it indicates how ill-mannered we have become. This little book lays out a set of simple niceties that should be considered in every household, not only for children but for adults as well: after all, we were the ones who first did the forgetting.

It so happens that most of the rules of society are prohibitory in character. This fact undoubtedly suggested the negative form originally adopted in this book and permitted the various injunctions to be expressed in a sententious and emphatic manner.

Many of the rules here given were drawn from established authorities of the time, but a considerable number of them were explained to be the result of the compiler's personal observation and experiences.

There are some persons, no doubt, who will condemn many things here contained as being unnecessary because they are generally known; but it was necessary to include familiar rules in order to give something like completeness to the list. Anyone who carefully observes, however, will note that nearly every rule given is frequently violated by persons of at least good social standing. These instances probably often occur through thoughtlessness or carelessness, but this book was intended to remind more than it was designed to instruct.

Foreword

Other critics may condemn some of the injunctions as over-nice. All that can be said in reply is that every person clearly has the right to determine for himself at what point below perfection he is content to let fall his social culture.

Eric Sloane
Cornwall Bridge
Connecticut

Don't

At the TABLE

Don't, as an invited guest, be late for dinner. This is a wrong to your host, to other guests and to the dinner.

Don't be late at the domestic table as this is a wrong to your family and is not calculated to promote harmony and good feeling.

Don't seat yourself until the ladies are seated or, at a dinner party, until your host or hostess gives the signal. Don't introduce (if you introduce at all) after the company is seated.

Don't sit a foot away from the table or sit jammed up against it.

Don't tuck your napkin under your chin or spread it upon your breast: bibs and tuckers are for the nursery. Don't spread your napkin across your lap; let it fall over your knee.

Don't serve gentlemen guests at your table until all the ladies are served, including those who are members of your household.

Don't eat soup from the end of your spoon, but from the side. Don't gurgle or draw in your breath audibly or make other noises when eating soup. Don't ask for a second serving of soup.

Don't bend over your plate or drop your head to get each mouthful. Keep as upright an attitude as you can without appearing stiff.

Don't load up the fork with food with your knife and then cart it away to your mouth; rather take upon your fork what it can easily carry and no more.

Don't use a steel knife with fish. A silver knife is now put by the side of each plate for the fish course.

Don't handle your knife and fork

awkwardly; let the handles rest in the palm of your hand. Don't stab with your knife or handle it as if it were a dagger.

Don't eat fast or gorge. Take always plenty of time. Haste is vulgar.

Don't take huge mouthfuls or fill your mouth with too much food. Don't masticate audibly.

Don't put your knife into the butter, into the saltcellar or into any dish.

Don't spread out your elbows when you are cutting your meat but keep your elbows close to your side.

Don't eat vegetables with a spoon, but use a fork. The rule is not to eat anything with a spoon that can be eaten with a fork. Even ices are now often eaten with a fork.

Don't devour the very last mouthful of soup, the last fragment of bread or the last morsel of food. It is not expected that your plate should be sent away cleansed by your gastronomical exertions.

Don't leave your knife and fork on your plate when you send it for a second supply. (This rule is disputed by the English. The logic of the question, however, proves the correctness of the rule, for it is not easy to place food upon a plate already occupied by a knife and fork It is always a law of politeness to incommode one's self rather than incommode others, so the problem of what to do with your dinner tools should be your own problem rather than that of the host's. The handles of knives and forks are now loaded so that the blades or tines will not soil the cloth when rested upon the table. Or one may with a little skill hold his knife and fork without awkwardness.)

Don't reject bits of bone or other substances by spitting them back into the plate. Quietly eject them upon your fork, holding it to your lips and then place them upon the plate. Fruit stones may be removed with the fingers.

Don't bite your bread; break it off with your hand. Don't trowel butter across an unbroken slice of bread.

Don't stretch across another's plate to reach anything.

4

don't *trowel*

Don't apply to your neighbor to pass articles when the servant is at hand.

Don't finger articles; don't play with your napkin or your goblet or your fork or with anything.

Don't mop your face or beard with a napkin. Draw it across your lips neatly.

Don't turn your back to one person for the purpose of talking with another; don't talk across the one seated next to you.

Don't forget that the lady sitting at your side has the first claim upon your attention. A lady at your side must not be neglected whether you have been introduced to her or not.

Don't talk when your mouth is full.

Never, in fact, have your mouth full. It is more healthful and in better taste to eat by small morsels.

Don't be embarrassed. Endeavor to be self-possessed and at ease. Remember that self respect is as much a virtue as respect for others; one should never be self-conscious.

Don't drop your knife or fork but if you do, don't be disconcerted. Quietly ask for another and give the incident no further heed. Don't be disquieted at accidents or blunders of any kind, but let all mishaps pass off without comment and with philosophical indifference.

Don't throw yourself loungingly back into your chair. The Romans lounged and did other things at table which modern civilization does not permit.

Don't lean or rest your elbows upon the table.

Don't use a toothpick at table unless it is necessary; in that case cover your mouth with one hand while you remove the obstruction which bothers you.

At the Table

Don't eat onions or garlic, which will offend others later. It is not desirable to carry with us unpleasant evidences of what we have been eating or drinking.

Don't press food upon a guest. This was once thought necessary and it was considered polite for a guest to continue accepting or to signify by a particular sign that he has had enough. (The Prince of Broglie, who traveled in our country in 1782, dined with "the lady of Robert Morris" and was repeatedly asked to have his cup refilled. When he had swallowed his twelfth cup of tea, his neighbor whispered into his ear and told him when he had enough of the water diet he should place his spoon across his cup else the hostess would go on refilling the cup and urging him to drink tea till the crack of doom.) To worry a guest with ceaseless importunities is now considered the worst possible taste.

Don't, as a guest, fold your napkin when you have finished. Place the napkin loosely upon your place at the table.

Don't fail at dinner to rise when the ladies leave the table, and remain standing until they have left the room. Then reseat yourself if you intend to remain for cigars.

Don't drink too much wine.

Don't thank host or hostess for your dinner. Express pleasure in the entertainment when you depart, and that is all.

Don't come to breakfast in deshabille. A lady's morning toilet should be simple but fresh and tasteful and her hair not in curl-papers. A gentleman should wear his morning suit and never his dressing gown. There are men who sit at a table in their shirt-sleeves; this is very vulgar.

Don't, as hostess, follow the English fashion and omit napkins at breakfast. The hardihood with which an Englishman attacks coffee and eggs without a napkin may excite our wonder, but how can the practice be defended? Is it anything less than disgusting?

Don't drink from your saucer. While you must avoid this vulgarity, don't take notice of it or any mistake of the kind when committed by others. (It is related that at the table of an English prince a rustic guest poured his tea into his saucer much to the visible amusement of the court ladies and gentlemen present. Whereupon the prince quietly poured his own tea into his own saucer, thereby rebuking his ill-mannered court and putting his guest in countenance.)

Don't carry your spoon in your tea or coffee cup.

Don't break an egg into a cup or glass but eat it from the shell. (This rule is not generally observed with us but it is universal in England, where an egg beaten up in a glass is considered an unpleasant mess.)

Don't read newspaper or book or letters at table if others are seated with you.

Don't be so careless as to decorate your shirtfront with egg or coffee drippings, or ornament your lapels with grease spots. Few things are more distasteful than to see a gentleman bearing

9

upon his apparel ocular evidence of having breakfasted or dined.

Don't rise from the table until the meal is finished.

Many rules of the table seem arbitrary to some persons, but they are the result of the mature experience of society. The object of a code is to exclude or prevent everything that is disagreeable, and to establish the best method of doing that which must be done. It is not necessary to point out that a dinner served and eaten in disregard of all rules would be a savage carousal; this being true, it ought to be seen that if rules to any degree elevate the act of eating, then a code of rules, generally observed, lifts eating to a still higher plane and makes it a fine art.

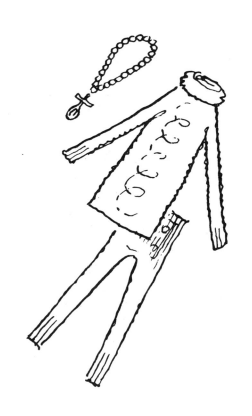

In DRESS and Habits

Don't be over-familiar in your habits. Don't strike your friends on the back, nudge them in the side or give other physical manifestations of your pleasure. Don't indulge in these familiarities and don't submit to them from others.

Don't bolt without notice into anyone's apartment. Respect always the privacy of your friends, however intimate you may be with them.

Don't leave any door open that you found closed or close a door that you found open. Don't slam a door or allow a door to slam of itself.

Don't neglect personal cleanliness— which is more neglected than careless observers suppose.

13

Don't wear soiled linen. Be scrupulously particular on this point.

Don't be untidy in anything. Neatness is one of the most important of the minor morals.

Don't neglect details of the toilet. Many persons neat in other particulars, for example, carry blackened fingernails. This is disgusting.

Don't neglect the small hairs that project from the nostrils and grow about the apertures of the ears. These are small matters of the toilet that often are overlooked.

Small *matters of the toilet.*

Don't cleanse your ears or your nose or trim and clean your fingernails in public. Cleanliness and neatness in all things pertaining to the person are indispensable but toilet offices are proper only in the privacy of one's apartment.

Don't use hair dye. The color is not like nature and it deceives no one. (Hair and beard dyed black produce a singular effect: they seem to coarsen and vulgarize the lines of the face. Anyone who has ever seen an elderly gentleman suddenly abandon his dye and appear with his gray locks in all their natural beauty will realize what is meant, for a coarse and sensuous face will have at once changed to one of refinement and character.)

Don't use hair oil or pomades. This habit was once quite general but it is now considered vulgar and it is certainly not cleanly.

Don't wear apparel with decided colors or with pronounced patterns. Don't (we address here the male reader) wear anything that is "pretty." What have men to do with pretty things? Select quiet colors and unobtrusive patterns and adopt no style of cutting that belittles the figure or makes it grotesque. It is right enough that men's apparel should be becoming and that it should be graceful but also that it should lend dignity instead of novelty to the figure. A man's figure or his costume should never be ornamental, pretty or capricious, except at a fancy-dress ball.

Don't wear fancy-colored shirts or embroidered shirt fronts. Spotted or otherwise decorated shirts are fashionable in summer but the choice is possibly questionable. White plain linen is always in the best taste.

Don't wear evening dress in the morning or on any occasion before six o'clock. (This is the English rule and is generally accepted here. The French, however, wear evening clothes on ceremonious occasions at whatever hour they may occur.)

Don't wear black broadcloth in the morning.

Don't wear your hat cocked over your eye or thrust back upon your head: one method is rowdyish, the other is rustic.

Don't go with your boots unpolished.

16

Rustic

Rowdy

Don't have your polishing done in the public highways. A gentleman perched on a high curbstone chair within the view of all passersby while he is having executed this finishing touch of the toilet presents a picture more unique than dignified.

Don't wear dressing gown and slippers anywhere but within your bedroom. To appear at table or anywhere in this garb is the soul of vulgarity. The dressing gown is garb for neither the breakfast room, the dining room nor the drawing room.

Don't walk with a slouching, slovenly gait. Walk erectly and firmly but not stiffly: walk with ease but still with dignity. Don't bend out the knees nor walk in-toed, nor drag your feet along. Walk in a large, easy, simple manner without affectation but not negligently.

Don't carry your hands in your pockets. Don't thrust your thumbs into the armholes of your waist-coat.

Don't chew or nurse your toothpick in public or anywhere else.

Don't chew tobacco. It is a bad and ungentlemanly habit. The neatest tobacco chewer cannot wholly prevent the odor of tobacco from affecting his breath and clinging to his apparel and the "places that know him."

Don't expectorate. Men in good health do not need to expectorate: with them, frequent expectoration is simply the result of habit. Spitting upon the floor anywhere is inexcusable, as is spitting on the sidewalk or into a fireplace. The English rule is to spit into a handkerchief, but this is not a pleasant alternative. It is often said that the excessive expectoration in America is due to the dryness of the climate; but if this is the case, how is it that the habit is confined to the masculine sex?

Spittoon
U.S.A. CIRCA 1845

Don't whistle in the street, in a public vehicle, at public assemblies or any place where it may annoy: don't, as a matter of fact, whistle at all.

Don't laugh boisterously. Laugh heartily when the occasion calls for it, but the loud guffaw is not necessary for heartiness.

Don't have the habit of "grinning" at nothing. Smile or laugh when there is occasion to do either, but at other times keep your mouth shut and your manner composed. People who laugh at everything are commonly capable of nothing.

19

Don't blow your nose in the presence of others if you can possibly avoid it. There are persons who perform the operation with the fingers but this disgusting habit is confined to people of the lowest class. Under any circumstance it is revolting to witness the performance however nose-blowing may be done. The Japanese think our custom of discharging offensive matter of the kind into a handkerchief and then stowing it away in our pockets is peculiarly disgusting. They discharge it into small bits of paper which they throw away.

Don't gape or hiccough or sneeze in company. When there is an inclination to hiccough or sneeze, hold your breath for a moment and resist the desire.

Don't have the habit of letting your lip drop and your mouth remain open. Breathe through your nostrils and not through your mouth. An open mouth indicates feebleness of character, while this bad habit also affects the teeth and the general health.

Don't keep carrying your hands to your face, pulling your whiskers, adjusting your hair or otherwise fingering yourself. Keep your hands quiet and under control.

Don't wear your hat in a strictly private office. This is no more justifiable than wearing a hat in a drawing room.

Don't carry a lighted cigar into a private office or into a sales room.

Don't pick up letters, accounts, or anything of a private character that is lying on another's desk.

Don't look over another person's shoulder when he is reading or writing.

Don't twirl a chair or other object while either talking or listening to anyone. This annoying trick is very common.

Don't beat a tattoo with your foot in company or anywhere to the annoyance of others. Don't drum with your fingers on a chair. Don't hum. The instinct for making noises is a survival of savagery.

Don't be servile toward superiors or arrogant toward inferiors. Maintain your dignity and self-respect in the one case and exhibit a regard for the feelings of people, whatever their station may be, in the other.

Don't be a "swell" or a "dude" or whatever the fop of the period is called.

a Fop...
c. 1830

Don't borrow books unless you return them promptly. If you do borrow books, don't mar them in any way; don't bend or break the backs, don't fold down the leaves, don't write on the margins, don't stain them with grease spots. Read them but treat them as friends that must not be abused.

Don't be selfish; don't be exacting; don't storm if things go wrong. Don't be grim and sullen. Don't fret—one fretful person in a house is ruin to its peace; don't make yourself in any particular a nuisance to your family or your neighbor.

Don't go into the presence of ladies with your breath redolent of wine or spirits, or your beard rank with the odor of tobacco. Smokers should be careful to wash the mustache and beard after smoking.

Don't drink wine or spirits in the morning or at other times than dinner.

Don't frequent bar rooms. Tippling is not only vulgar and disreputable but injurious to the health.

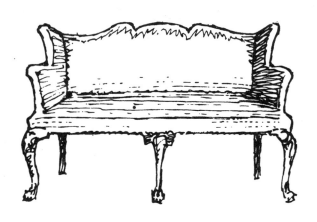

In the
DRAWING
ROOM

Don't, however brief your call, wear your overcoat or overshoes into a living room. If you are making a short call, carry your hat and cane in your hand but never bring an umbrella into the drawing room.

Don't attempt to shake hands with everyone present. If host or hostess offers a hand, take it; a bow of acknowledgement is sufficient for the rest.

Don't, in any case, offer to shake hands with a lady: the initiative must always come from her. By the same principle don't offer your hand to a person older than yourself, or to anyone whose rank may be supposed to be higher than your own until he has extended his.

Don't, as hostess, insist upon taking a caller's hat or cane. Pay no attention to these articles; it is right that he should carry them and it is incorrect that you should take notice of them.

Don't be in a precipitate hurry to get into a chair. It is just as graceful and easy and as proper to stand; it is easier to converse (as public speakers have noticed) when in that attitude.

Don't be cold and distant; don't on the other hand be gushing and effusive. A cordial yet quiet manner is the best.

Don't stare at the furniture, at pictures or other objects; of course, don't stare at people present.

Don't fail to rise, if you are seated, whenever a lady enters a room.

Don't stretch yourself on the sofa or in an easy chair. Don't lounge anywhere except in your own apartment.

Don't sit cross-legged. Pretty nearly everybody of the male sex does, but nevertheless don't you do it.

Don't sit with your chair resting on its

hind legs. Keep quiet and at ease in your chair.

Don't keep shifting your feet about, twirl your thumbs or play with tassels or knobs. Cultivate repose.

Don't be self-conscious. True politeness is always so busy in thinking of others that it has no time to think of itself.

Don't, in introducing, present ladies to gentlemen; gentlemen should be presented to ladies. Young men should be presented to elderly men and not in the reverse; young women to elderly women.

Don't, when asked to sing or play, refuse, unless you really intend not to perform. To refuse simply in order to lead your hostess on to repeated importunities is an intolerable exhibition of vanity and caprice. To every hostess therefore, we say:

Don't ask anyone more than once after a first refusal to sing or play.

Don't play the accordion, the violin, the piano or any musical instrument to excess. Your neighbors have nerves and need at times a little relief from inflictions of any kind. If you could manage not to play on instruments at all, unless you are an accomplished performer, so much the better.

Don't touch people when you have occasion to address them. Catching people by the arms or the shoulders or nudging them to attract attention is a violation of good breeding.

Don't talk over-loud or try to monopolize the conversation.

Don't talk to one person across another, but move into a proper position.

Don't whisper in company. If what you wish to say cannot be spoken aloud, reserve it for a suitable occasion.

Don't talk about yourself and don't talk about your affairs. If you wish to be popular, talk to people about what interests them and not about what interests you.

Don't talk in a social circle to one person of the company about matters that solely concern him and yourself, or which you and he alone understand.

Don't talk about maladies, or about your afflictions or other troubles. A complaining person is at once a pronounced bore.

Don't talk about people unknown to those present.

Don't be witty at another's expense or

ridicule anyone. Don't infringe in any way upon the harmony of the company. Although the exact definition of a gentleman might vary, the most common basic is that he is one who never takes advantage of another person or acts at the expense of another.

Don't ever, but ever, repeat scandals and malicious rumors of the hour.

Don't discuss equivocal people or broach topics of questionable propriety.

Don't (this by way of suggestion) dwell on the beauty of women not present, on the splendor of other people's houses, on the success of other people's entertainments. Excessive praise of people or things elsewhere is apt to imply discontent with people or things present.'

Don't fail to exercise tact. If you have not tact, you at least can think first about others and next about yourself, and this will go a good way toward becoming tactful.

Don't introduce religious or political topics in miscellaneous gatherings. Discussions on these subjects are very apt to cause irritation, hence it is best to avoid them.

Don't give a false coloring to your statements. Truthfulness is largely a matter of habit. Where very few people would deceive or lie maliciously, many become wholly untrustworthy on account of their habit of exaggeration and added coloring.

Don't interrupt. To cut a person short in the middle of his story is unpardonable.

to cut a conversation is unpardonable

Don't contradict. Difference of opinion is no cause of offense, but downright contradiction is a violation of one of the canons of good society.

Don't be disputatious. An argument

which goes rapidly from one to another may be tolerated; but when two people in company fall into a heated dispute, to the exclusion of all other topics, the hostess should arbitrarily interfere and banish the theme.

Don't be long-winded when you have a story to tell. Do not go into every detail and branch off at every word—be direct, compact, clear, and get to the point as soon as you can.

Don't cling to one subject. Don't talk about matters that people generally are not interested in; don't, in short, be a bore.

Don't repeat old jokes or tell time-worn stories. Don't make obvious puns. An occasional pun, if a good one, is a pleasing thing; but a ceaseless flow of puns is simply maddening.

Don't repeat anecdotes, good or bad. A very good thing becomes foolishness or very trying to the ears of a listener after hearing it several times.

Don't respond to remarks made to you

with mere monosyllables. This is chilling if not fairly insulting. Always have something more to say than one word.

Don't say "huh?" for "what did you say?" or "uh hunh" for "yes." Grunting sounds indicating "yes" or "no" are beneath the dignity of human communication or they might suggest an extremely limited vocabulary.

Don't appear listless and indifferent or exhibit impatience when others are talking. Listening politely to everyone is a cardinal necessity of good breeding.

Don't be conceited. Don't dilate on your own requirements or achievements; don't expatiate on what you have done, what you are going to do, or hint of your superior talents.

Don't always make yourself the hero of your own stories.

Don't show a disposition to find fault or to deprecate. Indiscriminate praise is nauseating; but on the other hand indiscriminate condemnation is irritating. One should develop a keen sense of the merits of a thing and an equally keen sense of its faults.

Don't be sulky because you imagine yourself neglected. Think only of pleasing and try constantly to please.

Don't show repugnance, even to a bore. A supreme test of politeness is submission to various social afflictions without a wince.

Don't, when at the card table, moisten your thumb and fingers at your lips in order to facilitate the dealing of the cards. This common habit is very vulgar. The aristocratic circles of a European court were much horrified a few years ago with the practice of this trick by the American ambassador.

Don't show ill temper if the game goes against you.

Don't fail in proper attention to elderly people. Young persons are often scandalously neglectful of the aged, especially if they are deaf or otherwise afflicted. Nothing shows a better heart or a nicer sense of true politeness than kindly attention to those advanced in years.

Don't in company inspect books or begin reading to yourself. If you are tired of the company, withdraw; if not, honor it with your whole attention.

Don't stand before the fire to the exclusion of the warmth from others.

Don't, in entering or leaving a room with ladies, go before them. They should have precedence always.

Don't keep looking at your watch as if you are impatient for the time to pass.

Don't scold your children or your servants before others. Respect their amour propre.

Don't bring children into company.
Don't set them at table where there are
guests. Don't force them on people's
attentions.

Don't as master or mistress give your
order in an authoritative manner; the
feelings of those under you should be
considered. You will obtain more willing
obedience if your directions have as little
as possible of the tone of command. Don't
trouble people with your domestic mishaps, with accounts of your rebellious
servants or with complaints of any kind.

Don't be that intolerant torment—a
tease. The disposition to worry children,
cats and dogs simply displays the rest-
lessness of an empty mind.

Don't wear out your welcome by too
long a stay; on the other hand, don't
break up the company by a sudden and
premature departure. A little observation
and good sense will enable you to detect
the right time to say "good night."

Don't make departure a major event of
the evening. Hovering at the threshold to
recount the reception, or to make future

arrangements, is always a boring exhibition. The most gracious exit is one without fanfare.

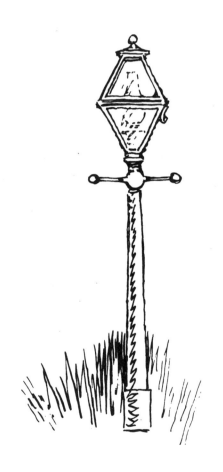

In PUBLIC Places,

Don't neglect to keep to the right of the promenade, otherwise there may be collisions and much confusion.

Don't brush against or elbow people, or in any way show a disregard.

Don't fail to apologize if you tread upon or stumble against anyone, or if you cause inconvenience in any way.

Don't stare or laugh at any peculiarity of manner or dress. Don't point at persons or objects. Don't turn and look after people that have passed.

DON'T

Don't carry your cane or umbrella horizontally. This trick in a crowd is a most annoying one to the victims.

Don't smoke in the streets unless on unfrequented thoroughfares. Don't smoke in public vehicles, and don't smoke anywhere that it might be offensive to anyone. Wherever you do indulge in a cigar, don't puff smoke toward the face of anyone.

Don't expectorate on the sidewalk but go to the curbstone to discharge excess saliva. Men who eject great streams of tobacco-juice on the sidewalk or on the floors of public vehicles ought to be driven from civilized society.

Don't eat fruit or anything in the public streets. A gentleman on the promenade engaged in munching an apple or a pear presents a more amusing than edifying spectacle.

Don't Smoke or Eat in the Street.

Don't obstruct the entrance to churches, theatres or assemblies. Don't stand before hotels or other public places and stare at passers-by. This is a most idle and insolent habit.

Don't stop acquaintances and stand in the center of the sidewalk so that others are forced from their paths. On such an occasion, draw your acquaintance to one side.

Don't forget to raise your hat to every lady acquaintance you meet, and to every gentleman you salute when he is accompanied by a lady. When with an acquaintance who raises his hat to another, you do likewise, although you might not know the lady he has saluted.

Don't stop a lady acquaintance in her tracks to speak with her, but turn and walk by her side; then leave her with raised hat when you have done.

Don't remove your glove when you wish to shake hands, or apologize for not doing so. It is entirely proper to offer the hand gloved.

Don't neglect to raise your hat to a strange lady if you have occasion to address her. If she drops her handkerchief and you pick it up for her, if you pass her fare in an omnibus or do any other small service, it should be accompanied by a distant, respectful salutation.

Don't be in haste to introduce. Be sure that it is mutually desired before presenting any one person to another.

Don't, in a walk, introduce your companion to every person you may chance to meet along the way. Off-hand street introductions are rarely called for and commonly they serve no end. ("It is the bane of social life in America," says a British correspondent, "that you are continually introduced to people about whom you care nothing and whom you do not care to know unless you are a railway-conductor or a reporter. One's hat, in America, is seldom on one's head.")

"One's hat is seldom on one's head."

Don't ask questions of strangers indiscriminately. Young women run risks in approaching unknown people with questions and they should scrupulously avoid doing so. In traveling, inquire of the conductor or coachman; in the street, wait until a policeman can be found.

Don't be over-civil. Do not let your civility fall short but over-civility is also a mistake. Don't rush to pick up a man's hat; don't pick up any article that a stranger has dropped unless there are special reasons for doing so. Be prompt to pick up anything a lady lets fall and extend this same politeness to elderly or infirm men.

Don't rush for a seat in a coach or at a public entertainment. If one should lose his seat due to the inconsideration of another, he would have the consolation of standing much higher in his own esteem —which is something most worthwhile.

Don't occupy more space in an omnibus than you require. In this particular, women are greater sinners than men.

Don't enter a crowded omnibus or

street-car. There doubtless are occasions when one cannot help doing so, but many times the vehicle that follows will afford sufficient room. ("The manners of the American people in public vehicles," a newspaper comments, "seem daily to be growing worse: if they decline, it will be nearly impossible for ladies or even gentlemen to enter them at all. The first thing one encounters nowadays, in a public conveyance, is a lazy fellow with his legs outstretched while perhaps a puff of smoke is blown into your face. Such a fellow should be promptly lodged in the street but he usually seems to be under the protection of the conductor, an official whose apparent business it is to give moral support to all the loafers who take pleasure in inconveniencing travelers. One is compelled to listen to idiotic whistlers and other noise-makers, and his emergence from the vehicle is accomplished only by a struggle with the boors that congregate on the platform.")

Don't bustle into a theatre or concert after the performance has begun, to the annoyance of others. The manager who will resolutely refuse permission for anyone to enter an auditorium after the curtain has risen will win for himself a golden meed of praise.

Don't talk at a theatre or at a concert when the performance is going on. To disturb others who wish to listen is gross ill-breeding. But unfortunately it is common with every class who pretend to an exclusive share of good breeding.

Don't, at any public entertainment, make a move to leave the auditorium before the performance is over. Men who recklessly and selfishly disturb public assemblies in this way have the instincts of animal society, not that of gentlemen.

Always wait for . . . .

the
END.

in Speech and Writing

Don't speak ungrammatically. Study books of grammar and the writings of only the best authors.

Don't talk in a high shrill voice. Avoid nasal communication but instead let your voice extend from the chest. Learn to moderate your tone, speaking in a low register but never low enough to strain the ears of your listener.

Don't use slang. There is certain slang (according to some) known as "gentleman slang," and other slang that is vulgar. If one does not know the exact difference, let him avoid using slang completely and then he will be safe.

Don't use profane language anywhere. Don't multiply epithets and adjectives and don't be too fond of superlatives. Moderate your transports.

Don't use completely meaningless exclamations such as "Oh my!" or "By crackey!" or "My goodness!"

Don't interject "sir" or "madam" freely into your conversation. Never say "ma'am" at all. Young people should be taught to say, "Yes, Papa" and "No, Mamma" (with accent on the second syllable of mamma and papa). "Yes, Uncle," "No, Aunt" and so on. "Sir" is correct toward superiors, but it should, even in this case, be used very sparingly.

Don't use the prefixes "miss" or "mister" without the person's name.

Don't address a young lady or speak to her as "Miss Lucy," "Miss Mary," etc. This is permissible only with those very intimate. Address a young lady by her surname, except when it is necessary to distinguish a younger sister from an elder.

Don't clip final consonants. Don't say "comin'" or "goin'" or "singin'" or "dancin'." Don't say "an'" for "and." It is either quaint or careless.

Don't Americanize and adopt rustic

pronunciations such as: persition for position, pertater for potato, sentunce for sentence, ketch for catch, feller for fellow, winder for window, tomorrer for tomorrow or meller for mellow. Such mistakes are often made by people of only some education; therefore don't be careless and fall into that certain class.

Don't say "doo" for "dew" or "due." Don't say "dooty" for "duty." Remember to give the diphthongal sound of "eu" whenever it belongs: the perversity of pronunciation in this particular is singular. "A heavy doo fell last night," one rustic will say. "Deuw tell!" will come as the response from the other.

Don't drop your R. Say "arm" instead of "ahm," "warm" instead of "wahm," "government" instead of "govament."

Don't pronounce incorrectly. Listen carefully to the conversations of culti-

E C 8 !

vated people. You will find they do not mangle their words or smother them or swallow them: instead they are recognized by distinct enunciation. Enunciate!

Don't say "party" for "person" or "gents" for "gentlemen." These are inexcusable vulgarisms. Don't say "my lady" or "your lady" when you mean "my wife" or "your wife."

Don't say "right away" if you wish to avoid Americanisms. Say "immediately," "directly" or "at once." "Right away" makes no logical or grammatical sense.

Don't say "sick" when nausea is meant; say "well," "unwell," "indisposed."(Sick for ill is almost universal with Americans, yet ill is certainly a better word.)

Don't use incorrect adjectives such as "elegant" as in an "elegant piece of beef" or an "elegant scene." When you exclaim, "Incredible!" to a statement, you are calling the speaker a liar or at least one who is speaking beyond your belief.

Don't use extravagant adjectives. Don't say "magnificent" when a thing is only pretty, or "splendid" and "excellent" when another word will do. Extravagance in any form is never in good taste.

Don't use the word "hate" or "despise" to express mere dislikes. The young lady who says she "hates yellow ribbons" and "despises turnips" may have sound personal principles but she evinces a great want of discrimination in the selection of epithets.

Don't say that anybody or anything is "genteel": don't use that word at all. Say instead that a person is "well bred" or that a thing is "tasteful."

Don't say "yeh" for "yes," and don't imitate the broad English "ya-as." Don't respond to a remark with "Yes sir!" or "Yesserree!" or a prolonged exclamatory and interrogative "yee-ess!" This is rank Yankeeism.

Don't say "don't" for "does not." Don't is a contraction of "do not," and not of "does not." Hence, saying "he don't" is never permissible. Say "he doesn't" or "he does not."

Don't, in referring to a person, say "he"

51

or "she" or "him"; always mention the person's name. In a group, don't say "she thinks it will rain" but do say "Mrs. Smith thinks it will rain." There are men who continually refer to their wives as "she" and wives who are each married to a "him." This is abominable.

Don't say "lay" for "lie." It is true that Byron commits this blunder in his, "There let him lay!" but poets are not always safe guides. "Lay" expresses action, while "lie" expresses rest. You lay a pillow down and lie upon it.

Don't say "I am through" when you are announcing that you have finished with your meal. "Are you through?" asked an American of an Englishman when seated at table. "Through!" exclaimed the Englishman, looking around in an alarmed manner down to the floor and up to the ceiling. "Through what?"

Don't misuse the words "lady" and "gentleman." The indiscriminate use of "lady" and "gentleman" indicates a want of culture. Don't say "she is a good lady" instead of a "good woman," or a "good gentleman" instead of a "good man." The words "lady" and "gentleman" are never used for simply indicating the sex of a person.

Don't use the word "please" too much; it seldom makes proper sense or grammatical logic. Say, "Will you kindly oblige me," or "It would please me" or contrive some other equivalent.

Don't adopt the common habit of calling everything "funny" that chances to be a little odd or strange to your way of thinking. "Funny" can be rightly used only when the comical is meant.

Don't use "mad" for "angry." This has been denounced as peculiarly an Americanism, and indeed this is so; yet the word is employed in this sense in the New Testament and is occasionally found in old English authors. But in today's usage, animals or insane people become mad, while one simply becomes angry or annoyed with another.

Don't use a plural pronoun when a singular is called for. "Every passenger must show their ticket," illustrates a prevalent error. Or "everybody put their hats on." It should be "everybody put on his hat."

Don't say "blame it on him" but simply "blame him." The first form is common among the uneducated.

Don't use the word "got" where it is unnecessary. "I have got a book," or "I've got to go home" should be "I have a book" and "I must go home." The word "got" (usually unnecessary, and far from a pleasing word) is properly used as the past of "get."

Don't say "awfully nice," "awfully pretty" and don't accumulate bad grammar upon bad taste by saying "awful nice." Use the word "awful" with a sense of its correct meaning. Or better still, avoid it completely.

Don't say "loads of time" or "oceans of time," as there is no actual meaning to such phrases. Say "ample time" or "time enough."

54

Don't say "lots of things." A lot of anything means one separate portion of a certain part allotted. Lot for quantity is an Americanism we can do without.

Don't use the word "smart" to express cleverness, brightness or capability. This use of the word, which really indicates either scheming or fashionable tendencies, is very common; but it is not sanctioned by people of the best taste.

Don't habitually use the word "folks." Strictly the word should be "folk" (the plural being a corruption). To say "his folks," or "our folks" or "their folks" is as poor taste as it is incorrect.

Don't speak of this or that food being "healthy" or "unhealthy." Instead say "wholesome" or "unwholesome."

Don't say "donate" when you mean "give." The use of this pretentious word for every instance of giving has become so common nowadays as to be fairly nauseating. If one cannot give his church or town library a little money without calling it a grant or donation, let him, in the name of good English, keep his gift until he has learned better.

Don't pronouce "God" as if it were written "gawd"; or "dog" as if it were "dawg"; or "coffee" as if it were "cawfee."

Don't notice in others a slip of grammar or a mispronunciation in a way to cause a blush or to offend. If you refer to anything of the kind, do it with careful courtesy and never in the hearing of another person.

Don't conduct correspondence on postcards. A brief business message is not out of the way but a private communication on an open card is almost insulting to your correspondence. It is questionable whether a note on a postal card is entitled to the courtesy of a response.

Don't write notes on ruled paper or inferior paper. Don't use paper with business headings for private letters. Tasteful stationery is considered an indication of refined breeding: tasteful stationery means note-paper of choice quality but entirely plain. Monograms or initials are permissible but there should be no ornamentation.

Don't cultivate an ornamental style of

writing. Don't imitate the flourishes of a writing master; keep as far away from a writing master's style as possible. A lady's or gentleman's handwriting should be perfectly plain and wholly free from affectations of all kinds.

Don't fail to acknowledge, by note, all invitations whether accepted or not. Never leave a letter unanswered. Don't fail to acknowledge all courtesies, all attentions and all kindnesses.

Don't, in writing to a young lady, address her as "Dear Miss." The use of "Miss" without the name is always a vulgarism if not an impertinence. It is awkward no doubt to address a young woman as "Dear Madam" but there is no help for it unless one makes a rule for himself and writes "Dear Lady."

Don't, in writing to a married lady, address her by her Christian name. Don't, for instance, write "Mrs. Lucy Smith," but "Mrs. Charles Smith."

Don't omit from your visiting cards your title, Mr., Mrs., Miss or whatever it may be. (It is very common in the United States for gentlemen to omit Mr. from their visiting cards and sometimes young ladies print their name with no title; but the custom has not the sanction of best usage. In England a young lady does not commonly have a separate visiting card: her name is printed upon the card of her mother, with whom her visits are always made.)

For Womankind

Don't over-trim your gowns or other articles of apparel. The excess in trimmings on women's garments, now so common, is a taste little less than barbaric, and it evinces ignorance of the first principles of beauty, which always involve simplicity as a cardinal virtue. Apparel piled with furbelows or similar adjuncts, covered with ornaments, and garnished up and down with ribbons is simply made monstrous thereby, and is not of a nature to please the eyes of gods or men. Leave excesses of all kinds to the vulgar.

Don't use the word "dress" for your outside garment. This is American-English, and, common as it is, has not the sanction of correct speakers or writers. Fortunately, the good old word "gown" is again coming into vogue; indeed, its use is now considered a sign of high breeding.

Don't submit servilely to fashion. Believe in your own instincts and the looking-glass rather than the dicta of the nantua-makers, and modify modes to suit your personal peculiarities. How is it possible for a tall woman and a short woman to wear garments of the same style without one or the other being sacrificed?

Don't forget that a bonnet should be so constructed as to cast the features par-

Victim of
the
Tyranny of
Fashion

tially in shade, for the delicate half-shadows that play in the eyes and come and go on the cheek give to woman's beauty one of its greatest charms. When fashion thrusts the bonnet on the back of the head, defy it; when it orders the bonnet to be perched on the nose, refuse to be a victim of its tyranny.

Don't wear at home faded or spotted gowns, or soiled finery, or anything that is not neat and appropriate. Appear at the breakfast table in some perfectly pure and delicate attire—fresh, cool and delicious, like a newly plucked flower. Dress for the pleasure and admiration of your family.

Don't cover your fingers with finger-rings. A few well-chosen rings give elegance and beauty to the hand; a great number disfigure it, while the ostentation of such a display is peculiarly vulgar. And what are we to say when many ringed fingers show a neglect of the wash-basin?

Don't wear ear-rings that draw down the lobe of the ear. A well-shaped ear is a handsome feature; but an ear misshapen by the size and the weight of its trinkets is a thing not pleasant to behold.

Not pleasant to behold.

Don't wear diamonds in the morning, or to any extent except upon dress occasions. Don't wear too many trinkets of any kind.

Don't supplement the charms of nature by the use of the color-box. Fresh air, exercise, the morning bath and proper food will give to the cheek nature's own tints, and no other have any true beauty.

Don't indulge in confections or other sweets. It must be said that American women devour an immense deal of rubbish. If they would banish from the table pickles, preserves, pastry, cakes and similar articles, and never touch candy, their appetite for wholesome food would be greatly increased, and as a consequence we should see their cheeks blooming like the rose.

Don't permit your voice to be high and shrill. Cultivate those low and soft tones, which in the judgment of all ages and all countries constitute one of the charms of woman.

Don't give yourself extensively to the reading of novels. An excess of this kind of reading is the great vice of womankind. Good novels are good things, but how can women hope to occupy an equal place with men if their intellectual life is given to one branch of literature solely?

Don't publicly kiss every time you come together or part. Remember that public displays of affection are in questionable taste.

Don't use terms of endearment when you do not mean them. The word "dear" in the mouths of women is often nothing more than a feminine way of spelling "detestable."

Don't, on making a call, keep talking about your departure, proposing to go and not going. When you are ready to go, say so, and then depart.

Don't make endless adieux in leaving

friends. The woman who begins at the top of the stairs, and overflows with fare-wells and parting admonitions every step on the way down, and repeats them a hundred times at the door simply maddens the man who is her escort, be he her husband or lover. Be persuaded, ladies, to say "good-by" once or twice, and have done with it.

Don't forget to thank the man who surrenders his seat in the car or omnibus, or who politely passes up your fare. Thanks from a woman are ample compensation for any sacrifice a man may make in such cases, or any trouble to which he may be put.

Don't carry your parasol or umbrella when closed so as to endanger the eyes of everyone who comes near you. Don't, when in a public vehicle, thrust those articles across the passage so as to trip up the heedless or entangle the unwary.

Don't be loud of voice in public places. A retiring, modest demeanor may have ceased to be fashionable, but it is as much a charm in woman today as it ever was.

Don't nag. The amiability of women, in

view of all they are subjected to from unsympathetic and brutal men, deserves great praise, but sometimes—Let it not be written!

Don't, young ladies, giggle, or affect merriment when you feel none. If you reward a bonmot with a smile, it is sufficient. There are young women who every time they laugh cover their faces with their hands, or indulge in some other violent demonstration—to whom we say,

the
1700s